# INSECTS

# INVADERS

# "INSECTS"

## HOWARD AND MARGERY FACKLAM

### TWENTY-FIRST CENTURY BOOKS

BROOKFIELD, CONNECTICUT

Twenty-First Century Books
A Division of The Millbrook Press ny, Inc.
2 Old New Milford Road
Brookfield, CT 06804

**Library of Congress Cataloging-in-Publication Data**
Facklam, Howard.
    Insects / Howard and Margery Facklam. — 1st ed.
      p. cm. — (Invaders)
    Includes bibliographical references and index.
    1. Insect pests—Juvenile literature. 2. Insects—Juvenile literature. 3.
Arthropod pests—Juvenile literature. 4. Arthropods—Juvenile literature. 5.
Beneficial insects—Juvenile literature. [1. Insects. 2. Insect pests. 3. Arthropods.
4. Arthropods, Poisonous.] I. Facklam, Margery. II. Title. III. Series.
SB931.3.F33 1994
595'.20465—dc20                             94-25428
                                                              CIP
                                                                AC

ISBN 0-8050-2859-5

Printed in the United States of America

10 9 8 7 6 5 4 3 2

**Photo Credits**
Cover: Alfred Pasieka/Peter Arnold, Inc.; pp. 9, 47: The Bettman Archive; pp. 11 (all), 13, 17: E. R. Degginger/Photo Researchers, Inc.; p. 16: Hans Pfletschinger/Peter Arnold, Inc.; p. 19: Visuals Unlimited; pp. 21, 38: Scott Camazine/Photo Researchers, Inc.; pp. 25, 51: Jeff Lepore/Photo Researchers, Inc.; p. 28: J. H. Robinson/Photo Researchers, Inc.; pp. 30, 32: Tom McHugh/Photo Researchers, Inc.; p. 35: Ed Reschke/Peter Arnold, Inc.; p. 37: Jean-Loup Charmet/SPL/Science Source/Photo Researchers, Inc.; p. 41: Kenneth E. Greer/Visuals Unlimited; p. 43: Martin Dohrn/SPL/Science Source/Photo Researchers, Inc.; p. 45: Alfred Pasieka/Peter Arnold, Inc.; p. 52: John Burnley/Photo Researchers, Inc.; p. 55: Laurie Smith/U.S. Department of Agriculture/A.P.H.I.S.

# CONTENTS

# 1

# THE SCIENCE OF INSECTS

Insects invade our houses, our crops, our forests, our domestic animals, and our bodies. It is not always easy to live with insects, but it's impossible to live without them. Scientists say our planet could perk along without humans, but without invertebrates—the spineless creatures like insects, worms, and spiders—all the ecosystems would soon collapse. In every kind of habitat, insects are at work. Even those insects we think of as pests may be doing vital jobs that no other creatures can do to keep nature in balance.

Some insects carry pollen from one flower to another, and without this pollination, plants cannot produce seeds. Other insects help scatter the seeds. As scavengers, insects eat and help bury dead plants and animals. Like small plows, burrowing insects turn over soil, which mixes organic material and oxygen into it and helps it drain. Insects also serve as food for birds, fish, and many mammals, including humans. Since ancient times, people have eaten insects because they are rich in protein and easy to find. In Thailand, people eat bee larvae; in Colombia, roasted leaf-cutter ants are eaten like peanuts; and in India, green weaver ants are ground into a paste and served as a topping for curry. And from insects we take honey, wax, silk, and the ingredients for a variety of drugs and medicines. Insects, however, also destroy crops and spread diseases. More people have been killed by diseases carried by insects than by all the world's wars and natural disasters combined.

To stay completely clear of insects, you'd have to live on the ocean floor or in outer space. Insects of one kind or another have made themselves at home in almost every other habitat, including deserts, rain forests, mountain snow, salt marshes, bubbling hot springs, and even pools of petroleum. Long before the age of the dinosaurs, insects dominated the earth. They were the first animals to take flight. No other class of animals has adapted itself to extreme conditions as well as insects.

Seventy percent of all the animals on earth are insects. There are about 800,000 known insect species, which is more than all the other kinds of animals together. And scientists believe there are thousands more insects that have not yet been identified. To show how many insects there are compared to people, the *New York Times* once reported that "for every pound of us, there are 300 pounds of insects."

Despite the fact that insects are everywhere, entomology, the scientific study of insects, was slow to develop. The Greek philosopher Aristotle, who lived from 384 B.C. to 322 B.C., believed in spontaneous generation. This belief said that life springs from nonliving materials. Aristotle once wrote that "every dry body which becomes moist and every humid body which dries up breeds life." For thousands of years after Aristotle, people believed that some insects, worms, and other small forms of life arose from mud puddles and rotting flesh. People saw flies emerge from decaying meat, so they reasoned that the meat gave birth to the flies. It wasn't until 1668 that Francesco Redi, an Italian physician, decided to test the truth of spontaneous generation. He conducted the first experiments that proved the reason flies

*Francesco Redi, who in 1668 investigated the spontaneous generation of living organisms from meat. Even though the results of Redi's experiments were accurate, his work was not generally accepted. It took another 200 years before the existence of spontaneous generation was finally disproved.*

seemed to come from rotting meat was because they laid their eggs on it. Redi's experiments were also the first recorded experiments in biology done under controlled conditions, so their accuracy could not be in doubt.

Even after Redi's pioneering work, little scientific attention was given to insects except by the naturalists who collected and identified them. One of the earliest illustrated books on insects was written by naturalist Thomas Moffett in 1634. By 1806, the Entomological Society of London had been formed. This society encouraged British scientists to exchange their scientific papers on insects with scientists in other countries.

People may wonder why the careful classification of insects is important. Why, for instance, does a scientist need to know whether one flea has more hairs on its body than another flea? The answer lies in the fact that small differences can lead to big discoveries. Identifying the one species of mosquito that causes malaria, for example, made it possible to control the disease. And knowing the specific species of fruit fly that attacks citrus fruits made it possible to save citrus orchards from ruin.

Today, entomologists around the world continue to collect and identify insects, but they also work in a wide range of fields. Insect specialists look for environmentally safe ways to control insects. They use insects to study genetics. Drug companies employ entomologists who screen insects for useful drugs. Dr. Tom Eisner, an entomologist at Cornell University, says this kind of "chemical prospecting" has already turned up insects that produce cortisone, steroids, and some antiviral compounds. And many murders have been solved by forensic entomologists. These scientists use the insects present on a body to determine whether or not a person was killed where the body was found. They also use insects to determine how long the person was dead.

But what exactly is an insect? An insect is a six-legged animal that goes through a series of changes called metamorphosis. Some insects, such as grasshoppers, have an incomplete metamorphosis. When young grasshoppers, called nymphs, hatch from eggs, they look like miniature adults. They live in the same habitat and feed on the same food as adult grasshoppers. Other insects, such as butterflies, moths, flies, bees, and beetles, have a complete metamorphosis and go through dramatic changes. They hatch from eggs into larvae that look nothing like the parents. The larva of a moth or butterfly is a caterpillar. A beetle egg hatches into a thick larva called a grub, and a mosquito hatches into a wriggler that usually hangs upside down in the water.

In some insects, the larva can be the worst invader because all it does is eat and grow. The adult clothes moth

*The complete metamorphosis of a butterfly. The black caterpillar, or larva, changes into a pupa called a chrysalis. The chrysalis remains in its cocoon until it has developed into an adult, at which time it emerges as a butterfly.*

doesn't eat a thing during its short lifetime, but its larva chomps like an eating machine through fur, feathers, and other natural fibers such as cotton and wool. Tent caterpillars can destroy a tree in a few days by eating all the leaves, but the adult moths do no damage at all.

After a larva has grown as much as it can, it changes again. In the case of a moth or butterfly, the caterpillar becomes a pupa, called a chrysalis, in a cocoon. The motionless pupa is never an invader. It does not eat. In this dormant, or resting, stage, the insect makes its most dramatic change into an adult moth or butterfly.

Spiders, ticks, lice, mites, and scorpions are often mistaken for insects, but they are really eight-legged animals that belong to a group called the arachnids. Insects and arachnids are close cousins. Together they belong to a larger group, the arthropods, which includes all the animals that have jointed legs and a tough outer covering called an exoskeleton.

Out of this huge group of insects and arachnid invaders, only a few are dangerous to humans. Some insects and arachnids bite. Others inject or spray venom. Some carry disease organisms into plants, animals, and humans. Still others burrow themselves directly into our bodies or into other animals or plants.

Ask any ten people what creatures they fear most and a majority will probably say spiders, wasps, or bees. On a warm summer afternoon, if a wasp cruises over a picnic table, people will often swat at it, scream, or run away, afraid of being stung. It's true that the wasp can inject venom with its stinger, but wasps don't have venom for the purpose of hurting people. Insects and arachnids were using venom to defend themselves and catch food long before humans appeared on earth. People get stung or bitten only when they get in the way.

In general conversation we use the words *poison*,

*venom*, and *toxin* to mean the same thing, but there are differences. A poison is a substance that in small amounts can cause serious injury or death. Many substances are harmful in large amounts, but not in small amounts. It is the dose that determines whether or not they are poisons.

A toxin is any poison made by a living organism—plant, animal, bacteria, or virus. Sometimes a toxin is called a biotoxin to distinguish it from a chemical toxin made in a laboratory. Venom is a toxin made by some animals, including snakes, spiders, and insects. The venom is passed to a victim by a sting or bite.

Technically there is a difference between an animal that is venomous and one that is poisonous. A venomous animal

*A wasp attacking an insect called a cicada. Because of the poisonous venom injected through the wasp's stinger, it can prey on animals larger than itself.*

manufactures and injects a toxic substance. A rattlesnake is venomous. It injects its venom through fangs. A wasp is venomous. It injects venom with a stinger. A spider is venomous because venom enters the victim when the spider bites it. But a poisonous animal is one that causes damage when it is eaten because its flesh contains a toxic substance. For example, it is safe to eat rattlesnake meat, as long as you don't eat the venom gland. But it's dangerous to eat a fish that contains a toxin in its tissues.

Venoms are commonly put in two general categories. Neurotoxic venom affects the nervous system and destroys nerve tissue. It kills by shutting down the nerves that control an animal's heart and lungs. Hemotoxic venom kills by breaking down an animal's tissues and destroying its blood vessels and cells. But venoms are complex substances, and some can be both hemotoxic and neurotoxic. In addition, each animal's venom is unique, with special components and properties all its own.

# 2
# THE VENOMOUS ONES

There are thousands of different kinds of wasps in the world. All of them have stingers, but most of them are harmless to humans. Even so, most people tend to avoid wasps, and if you know how these animals live, it's easier to stay out of their way. Social insects—those that live in large groups—are the only insects, and probably the only animals, that do not run away from humans. At all costs, they must defend their nest and their queen if they are to survive.

Yellow jackets and hornets are social wasps. They are easy to recognize by their yellow-and-white and black-and-white racing stripes. Yellow jackets usually live underground in old abandoned woodchuck and chipmunk burrows or in hollow logs. Paper wasps are hornets that build large paper hives in trees, in attics, under eaves of houses, and in other protected places.

Adult wasps feed on nectar and fruit juices. They don't make and store honey to feed their larvae, as bees do. Instead, they carry chewed-up chunks of fruit, insects, and rotting flesh, called carrion, back to the nest to feed their young. A yellow jacket cruising around your head may only be looking for tiny flies that swarm around people and other large animals. You can be sure that any wasps hanging around picnic tables and garbage cans are in search of meat and other scraps, and wasps cruising around fruit trees are looking for ripe fruit. They are not hunting for human victims. They sting people only to defend themselves.

Social wasps generally just tend to their business of finding food. But when their nest is disturbed, watch out! Anyone who has knocked down a hornet's paper hive or stumbled into a yellow jacket hole can tell you that the wasps swarm out like a squadron of fighter jets on the attack.

A wasp's stinger is a sharp sword that is kept in a sheath

*Paper wasps on their hive. These social wasps build their hive of coarse, papery material prepared by chewing wood fibers. The hive usually hangs from a tree branch.*

inside the wasp's body. During an attack, the stinger is unsheathed, and it can pierce skin as easily as a hypodermic needle. When a wasp pushes its stinger deep into flesh, muscles around the poison sacs squeeze venom into the wound. The wasp can pull out its smooth stinger and plunge it into its victim

*The unsheathed stinger of a hornet. The hornet has a painful sting, and its venom causes a very painful wound.*

again and again. But it's not the stings that cause the most pain. It is the venom, which is a combination of neurotoxins, hemotoxins, and several other components.

People react differently to a wasp's venom, but usually there is some swelling followed by itchiness. The itchiness can be soothed with a paste of dampened baking soda or meat tenderizer. First-aid manuals also suggest putting ice on the wound to help dull the pain and keep the venom from spreading. People who are sensitive or allergic to the venom can go into shock. They may have trouble swallowing. They may gasp for breath and feel dizzy. If such a severe reaction goes untreated, the person may die. People who know they have this dangerous allergy are advised to carry an emergency kit containing a syringe loaded with an antihistamine that can be injected immediately if they are stung. An antihistamine is a drug that stops the symptoms of an allergic reaction.

How do you keep from being stung? Don't walk barefoot through fields where yellow jackets might build an underground nest. When walking in any kind of wasp territory, don't wear cologne, perfume, hair spray, or suntan lotion that is heavily scented because the scent tends to attract these insects. Wear tan, white, or other light-colored clothes, which are less attractive to wasps than bright colors. Seal garbage bags and clean up around picnic areas so there are no scraps for wasps to feed on. But most important of all, don't panic if you see a wasp. Don't wave your arms around and swat at it, because these actions only make the insect more defensive. When a social wasp stings or is injured, it gives off a chemical message called a pheromone that signals the other wasps to join the fight against the enemy. This is why wasps suddenly seem to appear out of nowhere.

Solitary insects, which live alone, are less likely to sting people because they have no nest to defend. But like most other insects, a female solitary wasp's mission in life is to find a safe place to lay her eggs. She must also find a source of meat that will stay fresh for her newly hatched young to feed on until they become adults. No natural refrigeration exists to keep meat fresh for these larvae, but nature has come up with some amazing solutions.

The female tarantula hawk wasp is the biggest of the solitary wasps, and she is a fearless invader. Most solitary wasps lay their eggs on live caterpillars that cannot fight back. But not the hawk wasp. The targets for her eggs are huge, juicy tarantulas. Even though a tarantula is many times bigger than a hawk wasp, the wasp drives her powerful stinger right into the spider. The sting paralyzes the tarantula, but does not kill it. Then the wasp drags the motionless tarantula into the burrow she has prepared as a nursery, and there she lays one egg on the spider's abdomen. That done, she seals up the burrow with mud and flies away to find another tarantula for another egg. As each wasp larva hatches from its egg, it feeds on the live, paralyzed spider until the spider dies and the new wasp is ready to break out of the burrow.

The sting of a tarantula hawk wasp is said to be one of

*A tarantula hawk wasp attacking a tarantula. Once the wasp stings and paralyzes the tarantula, the spider is buried in the wasp's burrow. There it faces eventual death as food for the wasp's developing larva.*

the most painful, but it is unlikely that you'll meet one of these wasps if you stay away from the desert territory of the tarantula.

Each year, about 40 people in the United States are killed by the stings of venomous insects, and about half of those killers are bees. Most of the 3,500 different kinds of bees in North America are solitary. It is the social honeybees and bumblebees that live by the thousands in hives or nests. But no bee, not even a killer bee, will sting while it is at work collecting pollen or nectar.

Honeybees are big business. They are needed to pollinate crops. In fact, they are so important to our economy that professional beekeepers rent out millions of bees each spring to farmers who own large orchards of fruit trees and fields of grain. Getting stung, however, is of little concern to a bee-keeper, just like getting a splinter is of little concern to a carpenter. It goes with the job. Even though they wear coveralls and face nets, many beekeepers have been stung often. But these frequent stings usually help the beekeepers develop immunity, or resistance, to the venom. And for added protection, before they open a hive, beekeepers often puff smoke into it, which calms the bees.

There were no native honeybees in North America until the first colonists imported them because they needed the honey and wax bees make. These first imported bees were a feisty German breed. They were not easy to handle, but the colonists eventually learned how to manage the aggressive bees. Most of our domestic bees now are a gentler, more easygoing breed from Italy, or mixtures of several different breeds.

Honeybees called killer bees were imported to South America from Africa in 1956. Some Brazilian beekeepers who wanted to improve their honey production imported the African bees to crossbreed with their established honeybees. These African honeybees make better honey and more of it than any other bees. They also leave for work earlier in the morning, beating other honeybees to the best pollen and nectar, and they are more resistant to diseases than other bees. But despite all their good points, the African honeybees earned themselves the name "killer bees" because of the speed and ferociousness with which they swarm from the nest to attack an intruder. Their ferocious reputation got a big boost from a 1970s horror film that featured killer bees on the rampage, stinging to death almost anything that moved.

Bees swarm for the purpose of forming new colonies. Killer bees tend to swarm more often than other bees, and by swarming they have moved northward from Brazil at a rate of about 200 miles (322 kilometers) a year. In 1990, when one swarm of killer bees crossed the Rio Grande into Texas, they were destroyed by federal authorities. But there is no way to keep bees from crossing invisible borders between countries or states. In Brazil, several hundred people have been killed by the killer bees' venom, and the bees have killed cows and horses that were tethered too close to the bees' hives. The U.S. Department of Agriculture has reported 140 killer bee

*A killer honeybee gathering nectar. When a worker honeybee finds a source of nectar, it immediately flies back to the hive and performs a "dance" to communicate the location of the nectar to other workers.*

attacks between 1990 and July 1993 when the first death was reported: an eighty-two-year-old man in Texas who was stung more than 40 times!

Guatemalan and Brazilian beekeepers have learned how to handle the aggressive African killer bees, but no one can predict how these killer bees will behave if and when they settle in the United States. Beekeeper and author Sue Hubbell points out that our climate, beekeeping practices, and bee diseases and enemies will all be new to the killer bees, and they may not survive. The killer bees may mate with other honeybees to produce a more mild-tempered breed. On the other hand, a 1994 report in the journal *Nature* suggests that these bees aren't likely to calm down anytime soon. To be safe, stay away from the hives of all wild bees.

Only the female honeybee stings, and she can sting only once. Her stinger is barbed, and once in the flesh, the stinger stays put. When the bee tries to pull it out, her body tears away because the barbed stinger holds fast. The bee can't survive such damage, and she dies. If you are stung by a honeybee, don't try to pull out the embedded stinger. As you squeeze it between your fingers or with tweezers, you are likely to squeeze the muscles around the venom gland and force more poison into the wound. It is best to scrape the stinger out with your fingernail or the edge of a dull knife. First-aid manuals also suggest soothing the wound with a paste of wet baking soda or ice wrapped in a cloth. A pack of wet mud or meat tenderizer will also make the wound feel better.

It is all too easy to stumble upon bumblebees because they live in underground nests. But it's only through such an accidental meeting that this fat, fuzzy bee will sting a person. And unlike the honeybee, the female bumblebee does not die after stinging once. She can easily pull out her smooth stinger and plunge it into her victim over and over. So don't walk barefoot through fields of clover where bumblebees might be at work, and watch where you step.

Ants are annoying, but only a few of them are dangerous. There are some 10,000 different kinds of ants in the world, and about 600 species live in North America. Like other social insects, ants never turn and run from enemies. They are instinctively programmed to defend their nest and their queen. As part of this defense, ants produce a venom that is primarily formic acid. Formic acid is a colorless, irritating liquid that is so strong it was once used to tan leather and dye fabrics. In small amounts, formic acid blocks the respiratory system of other insects and small prey. In larger amounts, it can be painful to humans and other vertebrates. Some ants sting to inject the venom, some bite so the venom gets into the wound, and others spray the formic acid directly at the enemy.

Each year, millions of people in the southern United States are stung by fire ants. Unless you get away from a fire ant mound quickly, you're likely to be stung more than once because the first ant to sting releases a pheromone. This chemical "help!" signal calls the other ants to action.

There are three kinds of fire ants native to the United States. They sting, but as one scientist puts it, there's nothing remarkable about them. That can't be said about the tiny, reddish brown tropical fire ants that came to the United States in the 1930s as stowaways on cargo ships from South America. These fire ants attack first with their powerful toothed jaws. Once they have a good grip on their victim, they jab in their stingers and release painful shots of venom. The ants eat almost anything—insects, especially other kinds of ants, as well as grains and other plants. Swarms of the ants will attack newly hatched poultry, newborn pigs and calves, and other helpless young animals. The ants' appetites are voracious. They store grain, but unlike any other ants, the tropical fire ants also store the remains of their animal victims in their huge nests. So if you see a field of dirt mounds two or three feet high, stay away. Those are the nests of tropical fire ants, and there may be hundreds of thousands of ants in one nest.

Harvester ants that live in the Southwest United States have a vicious sting that leaves an intense burning pain. The nests of these ants also look like big mounds, and you can recognize the nests because the ants keep the plant life cleared in a big circle around them.

The common little red ants found in the woods seem harmless, but one scientist who was studying them discovered otherwise. He and one of his assistants found a huge nest of these ants, and out of curiosity, they poked at it. That was a mistake. "We had to turn tail to," the scientist wrote, "for in a few seconds the ants covered us with an angry army, half stifling us with their spray of formic acid."

If you are stung by harvester ants or fire ants, or sprayed by huge numbers of red ants, doctors recommend first washing the wound with soap and water. Then apply an ice pack or a paste made of baking soda and water, which may ease the pain. Get to the doctor quickly if you feel dizzy or nauseated, or show any allergic reactions to the formic acid.

A caterpillar is one stage in the life of a butterfly or moth. Its only job is to eat and grow. Swarms of caterpillars can strip a tree of leaves in a day, but these huge groups of caterpillars also become food for hungry birds. Some caterpillars protect themselves from being eaten with colorful camouflage, some with terrible odors, and some with prickly hairs that inject a mild venom. The puss moth caterpillar, saddleback, and caterpillar of the Io moth have sharp, hollow hairs that sting you when you touch them. The end of each hair is barbed, and the formic acid venom is sent from a sac at the base of the hair. If you want to pick up one of these colorful caterpillars, wear gloves, or pick it up gently on the end of a stick.

**24**

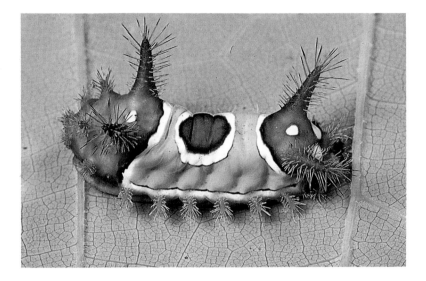

*A saddleback caterpillar moth. When touched, the stinging spines on the caterpillar's horns and sides release a venom, which deters predators from attacking it.*

The giant water bug is one of the largest insect invaders. Five species live in ponds, lakes, and streams in North America. The giant water bug is often called the "toe biter" because it may attack a person's bare toes that happen to be dangling in the water. The bug's bite is painful but harmless to humans, but it is deadly to other animals. This flat, oval, three-inch- (nearly eight-centimeter- ) long water bug can eat a whole fish, snake, lizard, frog, or other small animal. In a flash, a giant water bug can catch a frog with its powerful front legs, puncture the frog's skin with its sharp beak, and inject a venomous saliva that paralyzes the animal. The bug hangs on to its prey for a few minutes while the saliva digests the frog's body tissues and turns them to liquid. Then the water bug sucks out the frog's insides, leaving only the skin and bones.

# 3

# SPIDERS, CENTIPEDES, AND SCORPIONS

Even though most spiders are harmless, a lot of people probably think Little Miss Muffet did the right thing by running away when "along came a spider and sat down beside her." There was a real Miss Mouffet, who lived in France in the 1800s, and she had good reason to dislike spiders. Her father made her eat them! Thomas Mouffet was a doctor, and like all doctors in the 1800s, he had to rely on medicines made from herbs and other plants, or from parts of animals. Some people believed a whole live slug, quickly swallowed, would cure lung diseases. Others believed tea made from the ground-up brain of an owl would cure a headache. But Lucille Mouffet's father favored spiders. When little Lucille was sick, Dr. Mouffet gave her smashed spiders spread on toast for breakfast, which would likely turn anyone against these eight-legged animals.

Spiders are either trappers or hunters, but all of them are carnivores, which means they eat only meat. All spiders have venom, which is made in a pair of venom glands that leads to hollow fangs on their jaws. But most spiders are so small, and inject such tiny amounts of venom, that they are of no danger to humans.

Huge, hairy tarantulas, or bird spiders, may make

people nervous, but most of the 30 species of North American tarantulas do not have venom strong enough to kill a person. A tarantula's bite is painful because its venom is both neurotoxic and hemotoxic. The venom affects the nervous system and digests tissues, but usually the bite is not deadly. The sharp, barbed, stinging hairs on a tarantula's abdomen are irritating, too. Even so, several kinds of tarantulas have become popular pets because they are placid and interesting to watch, especially the Mexican Red-kneed tarantula and the Pink-toed tarantula from South America.

The black widow—just the name of this spider is enough to send chills through a person who is afraid of spiders. And well it might. So potent is the black widow's venom that at one time the Gosuite people of Utah mixed venom from this tiny spider with venom from a rattlesnake and tipped their arrows in it. But the Gosuites could have used the black widow's venom alone. It is 15 times more powerful than a rattlesnake's venom. The black widow's venom is also neurotoxic. It works quickly to paralyze the victim, usually an insect, before the spider sucks out the liquefied contents.

Even though they live in all the 48 mainland states, black widow spiders are not easy to find. The male is smaller than the female, and his jaws are too small to bite through a person's skin. The female is the dangerous one. She can be recognized by the red hourglass shape on her shiny black abdomen. Wherever people live, there are insects, and wherever there is a good supply of insects, the black widow spider might set up housekeeping. The female black widow weaves her free-form web in corners of barns, woodpiles, attics, sheds, and outhouses. Then she hangs there, upside down in her silk hammock, waiting for dinner to fly or crawl into her web.

Only when you go poking around in her hiding place will the female black widow bite you. And then you might not

*A female black widow spider, showing the distinctive red hourglass shape on her abdomen. The spider's neurotoxic venom is harmful, and sometimes fatal, to all victims of its bite.*

even know you have been bitten at first. The bite feels like a pinprick. But as the venom makes its way into your bloodstream, it sends agonizing pain from the site of the bite to the groin. Your legs begin to ache and the muscles of your legs and stomach become rigid. Some people say it feels like an attack of appendicitis. You might also experience nausea, sweating, shock, and difficulty breathing as the neurotoxic venom affects the nerve cells that control respiration. Still, only 4 percent of black widow bites cause death, and those deaths result from respiratory paralysis as the muscles of the chest grow rigid. A black widow bite is far more dangerous for young children than for adults because the dose of venom is comparatively larger for children. But such an experience is not pleasant for anyone. If you suspect you've been bitten by a black widow spider, get to a doctor as fast as you can.

The brown recluse is another small spider with a powerful venom. A recluse is a person or an animal that is not fond of company. The brown recluse spider likes to stay hidden. It doesn't go looking for someone to attack. Left alone, the spider would not be of danger to humans. Unfortunately, people get bitten because they poke their hands into cracks and corners where these spiders live. The bite of the spider is not very painful, just a quick sting. But in a few hours the pain begins in earnest as the area swells and turns red or black-and-blue. The real damage begins as the hemotoxic venom digests the tissue around the bite until it becomes an open sore that takes weeks to heal. Anyone bitten by a brown recluse spider must get to a doctor immediately.

Centipedes are named for their 100 legs, although they really don't have that many. True centipedes have only 21 or 23 pairs of legs. Each pair is attached to one segment of their long, flattened bodies. On the first segment, the centipede has a pair of curved, hollow claws that are attached to a venom gland.

The inch-long house centipedes that scurry around basements and in and out of drains on their long, delicate legs may look creepy, but they are harmless to humans. Actually, they are helpful because they eat flies, cockroaches, and other annoying insects. But in the southern and western United States there is a centipede that reaches a length of six

*A centipede, which lives in the soil and captures prey with its "poison claws"—a specially adapted pair of legs with fangs.*

inches (15 centimeters). Its painful bite is enough to put a person in the hospital for a few days. The amount of venom injected is seldom enough to kill an adult, but an equal dose can be fatal to a child whose body is smaller.

The best protection against centipedes is to avoid them. Centipedes hide during the heat of the day and hunt at night. So if you're camping in an area where centipedes live, make sure you don't walk barefoot at night. Shake out your shoes, clothes, and sleeping bags. If you are bitten, wash the wound with soap and water, and soothe it with an ice pack or a cold, wet washcloth.

In old Westerns there was often a scene in which a scorpion was the villain. If the cowboy didn't shake out his boots before he pulled them on, he was likely to be stung by a scorpion that was resting in the toe. Or when a bank robber reached into a rocky crevasse where a sack of gold was hidden, swift justice was done when the robber was killed by the sting of a scorpion.

Most of the 1,200 species of scorpions live in warm, dry climates, and most of them do nothing more than dine on insects or small birds and mammals. They aren't in the business of killing outlaws or attacking unsuspecting humans. A scorpion hides during the day and hunts at night. It will only sting a person if it is stepped on, cornered, or caught in the person's clothing. And stinging isn't a scorpion's first response. A scorpion first captures its prey in its sharp claws. If that doesn't subdue the victim, the scorpion curls its tail over its back and gives a quick jab that injects venom through the stinger at the tip of its tail.

It would seem that the biggest, most evil looking scorpions would be the most deadly, but that's not necessarily so. One of the largest scorpions has a painful sting, but its venom is not powerful enough to kill a person. But the venom from a small scorpion that lives in the Sahara Desert has been

*A scorpion. The large claws, which are used to catch prey, are really a special pair of limbs. The stinger at the very tip of the tail may also stab a victim and inject venom.*

compared in strength to the venom of a cobra. One sting can kill a good-sized dog in seconds.

Long ago, Greek peasants had a way of treating scorpion stings. They would catch a live scorpion, drop it into a bottle of olive oil, and cork the bottle. Before the scorpion died, it would eject a stream of venom into the oil. The Greeks were convinced that when this mixture of venom and oil was rubbed on a scorpion sting, it would soothe the pain and lessen the swelling. Did it work? It seems unlikely, and now no one would rely on such a remedy. Today, the bite of a deadly scorpion is treated with a serum called antivenin.

Antivenin is made by injecting a series of small doses of a specific venom into a horse or some other large animal. The animal's immune system reacts by making antibodies in the blood. Each week for several months, an increased dose is injected into the animal until it is completely immune to the venom. When blood is drawn from the animal, the serum part of the blood is separated and becomes the basis for the antivenin. A person who receives an injection of antivenin is getting antibodies to fight the effects of the venom. This kind of serum is especially useful in India, Africa, the Middle East, South America, and the West Indies, where some species of scorpions have deadly neurotoxic venoms strong enough to kill humans.

# 4

# THE
# CARRIERS

For millions of years before humans appeared on earth, fleas had been living comfortably on other animals. But when people began to huddle together in caves and huts, fleas were even better off. They moved in with the humans, and they have hitched rides on them ever since.

The scientific name of the flea that lives on humans is *Pulex*, from a Latin word meaning "dust." In ancient Rome, people thought fleas were animated dust, and a French poet once called a flea "a speck of tobacco with a spring in it." Long ago in India, people believed fleas were sent by the gods to poke lazy people into action as punishment for their laziness.

Fleas, whether they live on humans, dogs, parrots, or other animals, have changed little in the millions of years they have existed because their structure is so well-suited to life on warm-blooded animals. A flea has a tough, flattened exoskeleton that looks like it was pinched in a vise. It is covered with spiny combs that keep the flea from falling off a scratching animal, and its helmet-shaped head can slip through fur as easily as a plow through a field of tall grass. With the strong double claws on its six feet, a flea can cling like glue to skin, fur, or feathers. But the most amazing thing

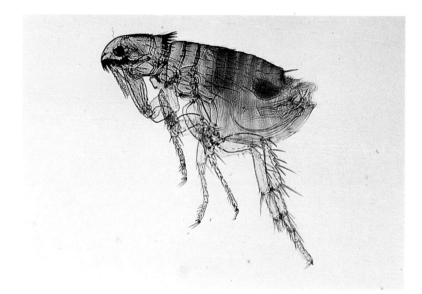

*A flea, typical of the type that lives on a cat or dog. A flea that usually lives on animals will attack a human only if it is very hungry.*

about a flea is the way it can jump. From a standing start it can jump 200 times its own length. (A flea the size of a full-grown person would be able to leap over a five-story building and land four city blocks away.) And a flea can keep on jumping for a long time. One flea-watching scientist counted 10,000 jumps in an hour.

It is this endurance and agility that have allowed fleas to survive so well. If the animal on which they are feeding dies, fleas jump off and on to the next animal that comes along. When you spray the fleas that are dining on your dog, for example, the fleas leap off and wait in floor cracks, carpets, or couches for another warm body to show up. It could be you.

Fleas are more than merely annoying. They can kill. One writer has labeled them the most efficient killers in history because they carry the bacteria that cause a disease called bubonic plague. During the Middle Ages, in the fourteenth century, bubonic plague earned a reputation as the Black Death because of the speed with which it swept through Europe. The disease killed 25 million people, which was about one-fourth of the population at that time. Earlier, in the sixth century, the same plague just about wiped out the Holy Roman Empire, when it killed 100 million people.

It wasn't until 1894 that anyone knew what caused bubonic plague; and even after the disease-causing bacterium, Pasturella pestis, was found, no one knew how the disease spread. Then in 1894, Kitasato, a Japanese scientist, discovered that the Oriental rat flea was the villain, the carrier of the bacterium.

People had lived with rats and fleas for so long that both pests were simply accepted as a part of life that couldn't be changed. Filth was common. The dirt fighters we take for granted now—vacuum cleaners, pesticides, flush toilets, detergents, hot and cold running water—did not exist. Garbage and human waste were tossed out windows. If garbage landed in the street, that's where it stayed. Rats were everywhere feeding on the garbage, and on the rats were fleas feeding on blood. In fact, fleas were so much a part of life that ladies of the English court wore fur collars in the hope that fleas would settle in the fur instead of on their skin. Books of etiquette described "popping" fleas and scratching in public as very bad manners.

A flea can carry the bacteria that cause bubonic plague from one rat to another or from rats to humans. The bacteria can also enter a victim in the bite of a flea. When a flea sucks the blood of a rat that is infected with bubonic plague, it also sucks up the bacteria that cause the plague. The flea gets so sick from the bacteria that it can't even swallow the blood it needs to live on. When the sick flea bites another rat or a

*A scene in the town of Marseilles, France, where an epidemic of bubonic plague broke out in 1720. People who were bitten by plague-infected fleas developed high fevers, chills, nausea, diarrhea, and enlarged lymph nodes, and often died.*

human, it spits up some of the infected blood into the wound made by its bite.

Today, bubonic plague is rare, but every once in a while a few cases of the disease break out in parts of the world where people are forced to live in overcrowded, unsanitary, rat-infested places. Much less rare, however, are some animal and human diseases such as Rocky Mountain spotted fever, Texas cattle fever, and Lyme disease, which are caused by one of the eight-legged pests, the tick. There are about 850 different kinds of ticks. They all live on blood, and they hang on tight as they take their time filling up on a blood meal. It has been estimated that in one summer, ticks may draw as much as 200 pounds (191 kilograms) of blood from a single cow or horse.

Ticks are successful because most of them have tough bodies covered by hard plates, and they have few enemies. They are so sturdy that they have survived for more than five years without food in a laboratory of the U.S. Public Health Service. And even more amazing is the fact that during that time the disease organisms stayed alive inside the starving ticks. A female tick infected with a virus or bacterium can even pass the organism along to her offspring.

All ticks go through four stages of development—egg, larva, nymph, and adult. Some kinds of ticks lay only 100 eggs, while others lay as many as 18,000. But all ticks have waxy-coated eggs that hatch into six-legged larvae called

*Two stages in the development of a deer tick. Of the two adults, the egg-laying female is the larger. The small nymph, which transmits diseases to humans, is actually only a little larger than the period at the end of this sentence.*

seed ticks. When these tiny seed ticks crawl to the end of a leaf or blade of grass, they wait patiently, with their forelegs stretched out, for days or even weeks. Alerted by the warmth and odor of an animal that brushes by close enough, a seed tick grabs on to the fur of the animal, which may be a mouse, chipmunk, rabbit, or other small mammal. The tick bites and drinks the blood of the animal, and when it is full, it drops off. Then the tick molts, which means it sheds its outer skeleton in order to grow. As a slightly larger tick, it again climbs onto a leaf or blade of grass and waits, this time for a bigger animal, perhaps a dog, deer, or human. If a tick happens to be infected with the one-celled organism that causes Lyme disease, called a spirochete, the tick passes the spirochete to the animal.

Ticks are in the news every summer because people go tramping through areas where ticks live. So how can you avoid ticks? When you walk through woods, brush, or tall grass, always wear socks, shoes or boots, and long pants with the bottoms tucked in to the socks or boots. Wear a long-sleeved shirt with buttoned cuffs and a snug collar, and keep the shirt tucked in. And spray an insect repellent containing a chemical compound called DEET on your socks, lower pant legs, sleeve cuffs and collar, and exposed skin.

Most people don't even feel the bite of a tick, so it's important to check your clothing when you return from walking in an area where ticks live. Before it digs in, a tick is easily brushed off, but the longer a tick is on your clothing, the greater the chance it will get on your skin and bite you. Once a tick bites and buries its head into your skin, it's there to stay. Take a shower to wash away any unattached ticks. Then search your body carefully because before feeding, a tick is only as big as a pinhead. If you find a tick, use a tweezers with a fine point to remove it. Put the tweezers as close to your skin as possible and on the tick's mouth parts. Do not pull at its head or body because it can break off easily, leaving the tick's mouth in your skin. Don't touch the tick. Remove it from the tweezers with a tissue or paper towel and wash your hands thoroughly. Then wash the area where the tick was and swab it with alcohol.

If you find a sore spot on your skin that looks like a bull's eye with red rings resembling a target or a red circle with a clear center, it may be where a tick is buried or has bitten you. Don't wait for other symptoms to develop. Go to a doctor immediately for a blood test that can accurately diagnose Lyme disease. The first symptoms of Lyme disease are like the flu, but if the disease goes untreated for a few weeks or months, Lyme disease can cause more serious, long-lasting problems such as crippling arthritis, abnormal heart rhythms, and in rare cases, neurological problems.

In 1994, the Centers for Disease Control and Prevention reported that about 10,000 cases of Lyme disease were reported each year in the early 1990s. Most of the cases were in the Northeast and northern Midwest states, which have the right combination for Lyme disease: rodents, ticks, deer, and what one scientist has called "woodburbs." Woodburbs were once wooded lands that were cleared and plowed for farming during colonial times. Eventually they became sub-urbs, and today many of these suburbs are once again sur-rounded by woodlands.

The good news is that a vaccine has been developed for Lyme disease. One place the vaccine is being tested is Block Island, Rhode Island, where as many as 1 in 20 people con-tract Lyme disease each summer. The vaccine works in two ways. It makes a person's immune system react as though it were being attacked by the Lyme spirochete, so the immune system produces antibodies that destroy the invader. And when a tick bites a person who has been vaccinated, it drinks the spirochete-killing antibodies along with the blood. The

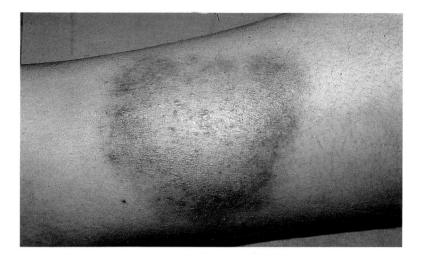

*A tick bite showing the very first stage of Lyme disease. If antibiotics are given when this bull's eye-shaped rash first appears, the person usually recovers quickly.*

antibodies then destroy the remaining spirochetes in the tick before they can be passed along.

Another insidious invader is the louse. A louse is a tiny, wingless, flat-bodied insect with claws that hold tight to hair and mouth parts that pierce skin and suck blood. The three kinds of lice that specialize on people are head lice, crab lice, and body lice. Head lice and crab lice are only irritating, but body lice can be life-threatening. During World War II, body lice were called cooties. Despite the funny name, cooties are no fun because they carry the deadly organisms that cause typhus fever. During World War I, an epidemic of typhus wiped out more than 150,000 people in Europe.

A body louse picks up the typhus organism when it bites a person who is ill with the disease. The organism multiplies in the louse's gut and is spread by the insect's excrement, not by its bite. The organism in the excrement gets into breaks in the skin when a person who has come in contact with the excrement scratches the area. The typhus organism can also get into a person's body through the mucous membranes inside the mouth or around tender eye tissues.

Typhus is rare these days. There is a vaccine to protect people who are forced to live temporarily in crowded, unclean conditions during wars or after natural disasters, and there are insecticides to get rid of body lice.

The tsetse fly is one insect invader people in North America don't worry about, but it is a continual problem in Africa. When the African tsetse fly bites animals and people, it leaves them with a disease commonly called sleeping sickness. A tiny one-celled organism called a trypanosome causes sleeping sickness. It lives in the blood of antelopes and other large African mammals, where it does no harm. But when a tsetse fly bites and drinks the blood of an infected antelope, the trypanosomes get into the insect's stomach. If the infected tsetse fly bites a person, the trypanosomes, mixed with the fly's saliva, get into the person's blood through the wound.

Trypanosomes can stay alive in a person's bloodstream for anywhere from a few weeks to a few years before they move into the person's lymph glands and finally into the nervous system. The first symptoms are swollen glands and a slight fever. They are soon followed by great sleepiness as the disease affects the brain and nervous system. It is a long-lasting, debilitating disease, and many people die from it each year.

In one effort to get rid of tsetse flies, thousands of antelopes in many African nations were destroyed by order of health officials, but that didn't stop the disease. The tsetse flies simply carried the trypanosome to other big mammals. It has not been easy to control the tsetse flies because there are 20 different species, and each species lives in a different

*A tsetse fly, the carrier of the organism trypanosome that causes sleeping sickness. In Africa, there are still about 25,000 new cases of this disease each year.*

habitat. Some congregate near water, some thrive in the flat, open savannas, and still others live in the rain forests. Even if the adult flies are killed by pesticides, their pupae can survive for long periods of time buried deep in damp, shaded soil.

Of all the insect invaders, mosquitoes seem to be the biggest pests. Mosquitoes have bugged humans for thousands of years, and today we don't seem to find any more good in them than our ancestors did. There are more than 3,000 species of mosquitoes. All of them are annoying, but only a few are really dangerous, and it is only the females of the dangerous species that bite. Both male and female mosquitoes feed on juice and nectar from fruits and flowers, but the females need a blood meal before they can lay their eggs.

For such a tiny creature, the mosquito has amazing power, especially in its mouth. The long, thin mouth part, called a proboscis, works like a straw armed with knife-sharp edges. The proboscis has six different parts called stylets, all encased in a single sheath that protects them. Each stylet has

**43**

a different purpose. One makes the incision. Another inserts an anticoagulant, which keeps the victim's blood from clotting and clogging up the mosquito's sucking stylet. Another adds digestive juices to the mosquito's saliva, and another is actually the straw that sucks out the blood.

The common mosquito, *Culex pipiens*, that buzzes around most backyards prefers to dine on the blood of birds, but it will also snack on dogs and people. It does not carry diseases. The harmful ones are the *Aedes* mosquito that carries yellow fever and the *Anopheles* mosquito that carries malaria. Mosquitoes have probably been studied more than any other kinds of insects because they carry this pair of deadly diseases.

Thousands of years ago in ancient Greece, the physician Hippocrates knew there was a link between malaria and stagnant marshy land, but he made the wrong connection. Like doctors for the next 2,000 years, Hippocrates blamed the foul night air from marshlands for the fever and chills that came with malaria. People who kept their windows closed at night got the right results even though they did it for the wrong reasons. In an effort to keep out the bad night air, they also kept out mosquitoes.

In 1878, the malaria organism was found in the blood of malaria sufferers. But the way it got there remained a mystery until 1898, when Dr. Ronald Ross proved that the *Anopheles* mosquito carried the disease. The bite of the female *Anopheles* is harmless unless the mosquito has previously bitten a person who has malaria and picked up the disease organism.

The same is true of the *Aedes* mosquito. If the tropical species of *Aedes* mosquito bites a person who has yellow fever, it picks up the virus that causes the disease. When that same mosquito bites another person, it injects enough of the virus to infect the second person. Once infected with the

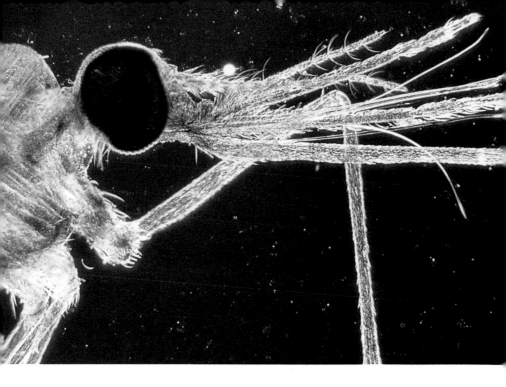

*The bloodsucking* Anopheles *mosquito, showing the six stylets of its proboscis. The mosquito only needs to feed on the contaminated blood of one person with malaria for the disease to be passed on to others.*

virus, the mosquito can pass the virus along to every person it bites. It is a carrier as long as it lives.

In eight years during the building of the Panama Canal, 50,000 laborers died from yellow fever, malaria, and plague. The French had started building the canal, but they gave up the project and turned it over to the United States in 1904, partly because so many of their workers had died from malaria and yellow fever. Immediately the surgeon general of the United States appointed Colonel William Gorgas to be in charge of disease control. Colonel Gorgas attacked mosquitoes every way he knew. He drained swamps where mosquitoes laid their eggs, poured oil on larger ponds to kill mosquito larvae, and cleared bushes and undergrowth where mosquitoes lived. He ordered screens put on the windows of buildings where workers lived and doses of quinine for everyone in the camps. Quinine was not a cure for malaria, but it eased the symptoms. At first people made fun of Gorgas. But by 1906, when he had wiped out yellow fever and rid the area of bubonic plague-carrying rats, people stopped laughing. By 1913, Gorgas had brought malaria under control in Panama, too.

Today the battle against malaria still goes on in some parts of the world. As long as there are *Anopheles* mosquitoes, even one person infected with malaria can start an epidemic.

One of the worst insect invaders is the screwworm fly. It is about three times the size of a housefly and a hundred times more disgusting. The screwworm fly does not carry a disease organism, but it does carry infections that can cause death. A housefly stomps around in filth and spreads whatever diseases it picks up, but the larva of the screwworm fly eats living flesh. The fly's scientific name, *hominivorax,* means "man-eating." During the Civil War, this awful insect infested and caused infections in the open wounds of soldiers lying on battlefields. But most of the time, screwworm flies concentrate their attacks on wild and domestic animals.

The female screwworm fly lays a compact mass of 200 or 300 eggs on raw flesh. The bloody navel of a newborn calf or lamb, a nick in the skin of a sheep just sheared of its wool, or any injury an animal cannot reach to lick clean is a target for screwworm flies. Within 12 to 24 hours, the maggots (larvae) hatch and begin to feed. They burrow into the animal's flesh head down, which causes more bleeding and attracts more flies to lay eggs. If the animal isn't treated, it will surely die.

Entomologist Edward Knipling is credited with finding a way to stop screwworm flies in Florida in the 1950s. He raised

*Workers building the Panama Canal. Because of unsanitary conditions and infestations of mosquitoes, thousands of workers died of mosquito-borne diseases such as malaria and yellow fever.*

the flies in a laboratory and exposed them to radiation to make them sterile, which meant they could not reproduce. The females mate only once, so Knipling's plan was to release sterile male flies to mate as usual. The female flies would still lay eggs. But the eggs would not be fertilized, so they wouldn't hatch. The first test took place on Sanibel Island, Florida, where there was a big population of screwworms. Within three months, the screwworms had almost disappeared from the island because no eggs were hatching. After another test on the island of Curaçao in the Netherlands Antilles, Knipling was ready to tackle a larger area in the southern United States. Over 18 months, a fleet of airplanes dropped more than two billion sterile flies on 70,000 square miles (182,000 square kilometers) of Florida, Georgia, and Alabama. As a result, screwworm flies were wiped out in southeastern United States.

But not for long. Since the screwworms were competing with an unnatural enemy, not a natural one, in the long run, the flies won. During the 1960s, the sterilized screwworm program saved millions of dollars worth of cattle in Texas. But in 1972, suddenly there were 100,000 infestations of screwworms. Scientists found that wild, untreated male flies were chosen by the females because they flew higher and more vigorously than the sterile, laboratory-raised males. Wild flies also searched out and landed on animals earlier in the morning and stayed active all day. The weakened flight muscles of the laboratory flies needed the higher temperatures of midday before they warmed up and became active. In competition with wild flies, the laboratory flies lost mating partners. In his book *The Dragon Hunters*, Frank Graham, Jr., wrote, "Once more the belief that man can single out an opportunistic alien species for complete domination was to be badly shaken." But entomologists have not given up. The research goes on.

# 5

# THE
# PLANT
# ATTACKERS

Gardeners, farmers, and foresters are constantly waging war against the pests that invade their crops—leaf miners, tent caterpillars, gypsy moths, weevils, fruit flies, corn borers, and hundreds of others. The insects, of course, are only making a living. Unfortunately, they are doing it in a habitat that happens to be supplying our food and other products.

Each insect specializes in attacking a different part of a plant in a different way. For example, there are grape rootworms, grape leafhoppers, grape berry moths, grape rootborers, grape mealybugs, grapevine aphids, grape leaf skeletonizers, grape flea beetles, grape leaf folders, grape cane girdlers, and a few other grape specialists.

There are about 40,000 different kinds of weevils, which are also called snout beetles. Each lives on a different kind of plant, but all the weevils have long, curved snouts that are equal to about half their body length. At the tips of their snouts are powerful cutting jaws perfectly designed to attack plants.

Aphids are known to transmit about 90 different plant viruses, and it takes an aphid only 30 seconds to spread a virus from one plant to another. A single swarm of millions of locusts can eat 20,000 tons of green plants in a day. And

Japanese beetles chew up some 275 different plants, causing millions of dollars of damage to farm and orchard crops.

For thousands of years, insects were limited to their home territories and were controlled by natural enemies in those territories. If the insects weren't carried by winds or migrating animals, they went only as far as they could fly or crawl. Today, however, insects move from place to place on jets, trucks, cars, trains, and cargo ships. The majority of the most injurious insects in any country have been imported by accident. These foreign invaders often do more damage than the native insects because their natural predators didn't travel with them.

One of the most famous insect invasions occurred in California in 1887 when a small, flat insect called the cottony-cushion scale almost destroyed the orange groves. These scale insects live in huge, flat, fuzzy-looking colonies. They suck leaves dry and spatter them with a waxy coating. At first no one knew where the scale insects had come from, but eventually they were traced back to shipments of fruits and vegetables from Australia. The clue to solving the problem of cottony-cushion scale came from the fact that these insects were *not* a big problem in Australia. There they were kept in check by a natural predator.

An American entomologist, Albert Koebele, was sent to Australia to bring back that predator, even though no one knew exactly what it was. What Koebele found busily eating the Australian cottony-cushion scale were vedalia beetles, also called ladybugs. Koebele knew it would be difficult to keep these ladybugs alive on the 28-day ocean voyage home. But he tried, anyway. He packed them on ice in the ship's meat locker, and the ladybugs arrived safely. It didn't take long for the little red-and-black beetles to make themselves at home in California, where they saved the orange and other citrus fruit industry by eating the cottony-cushion scale.

**50**

*A colony of cottony-cushion scale. The nymphs of this insect are concealed by long cottony fibers of wax as they feed on the juices from the leaves and stems of trees.*

Since then, ladybugs have proved to be one of the most helpful insects in the United States as they moved on to dine on many other plant pests.

There are dozens of stories about accidental insect invasions, but one of the most often told is that of the gypsy moth. A French naturalist, Leopold Trouvelot, imported some gypsy moth eggs to the United States in 1869 because he wanted to crossbreed the gypsy moths with silk moths. He kept the gypsy moth caterpillars on bushes covered by netting, but during a storm, the nets ripped and the caterpillars escaped. For ten years the gypsy moths gradually became accustomed to their new environment without becoming pests. But in 1882 a woman reported that gypsy moth caterpillars "were crawling over everything in our yard and stripped all our fruit trees." A man described the caterpillars as being "so thick on the trees that they were stuck together like cold macaroni." The gypsy moths were on the move, destroying thousands of acres of woodland. By the 1930s, however, the moths seemed to be causing less damage. Apparently some birds and other natural predators had found them and were holding them in check.

Then DDT was discovered, and huge areas of forest and suburban land were sprayed with this new chemical insecticide. Gypsy moths were killed off by the millions, but so were their natural predators. Enough gypsy moths survived the

*A gypsy moth caterpillar eating a leaf. The caterpillar eats the softer, juicier parts of a leaf first, and usually feeds at night. After about eight hours, the leaf is almost completely eaten.*

chemical spray to produce eggs for a crop of caterpillars the following summer. With fewer gypsy moths competing for food, these remaining caterpillars had plenty to eat. They thrived. And now, more than 100 years after gypsy moths were first imported into the United States, they have spread across the country.

Scientists today are still searching for the right predators to keep the gypsy moths under control. The newest research is focused on a fungus that attacks only gypsy moth caterpillars and a few closely related caterpillars. Microscopic spores from the fungus invade the skin of the caterpillar and devour it from the inside. Scientists expect a product containing this fungus to be available commercially by the year 2000.

Most entomologists agree that chemical insecticides are not the answer to controlling insect invaders. At best, they work for a while, but not forever. Insects either develop resistance to the chemicals or they adapt by finding new sources of food. Some things that work better than chemical insecticides are host-specific parasites, quarantines, bacterial and viral sprays, and pheromone traps.

Parasitic wasps are host specific. They lay their eggs in or on a specific insect, and when the eggs hatch, the larvae eat the host insect. In southern California, walnut aphids were destroying groves of walnut trees. A parasitic wasp known to kill walnut aphids was imported from France, and the wasp was successful in controlling the specific aphid that lived in southern California. But other aphids continued to thrive on walnut trees in central and northern California, so other kinds of parasitic wasps were imported that would specifically kill those aphids. This approach works well as long as scientists can continue finding specific aphids to match specific hosts.

People entering the United States by crossing the Peace

Bridge that spans the Niagara River between the United States and Canada must declare all fruit, vegetables, and live plants they are carrying. This is also true for people entering the United States from any other point in Canada, Mexico, and other foreign countries. Even passengers flying to the mainland from the state of Hawaii must pass through a plant inspection station when they land.

Why all this hassle over some fruit, vegetables, and plants? Because insects hide in or on them. For example, fruit coming into the country could have been invaded by a fruit fly. One fruit fly lays 100 or more eggs in a single piece of fruit. You might not even notice the tiny pinprick in an orange or a pineapple where a fruit fly inserted its eggs until you open the fruit to find a mass of squirming, white larvae.

The Mediterranean fruit fly, known as the Med fly, is one of the most destructive plant insects. The last big infestation of the Med fly attacked Florida fruit in 1956. Since then, quarantines have been used to keep this fly out of the United States.

Originally the word *quarantine* simply meant a period of 40 days, but gradually it came to refer to a 40-day period of isolation to prevent human diseases from spreading. Any ship from a foreign port suspected of carrying passengers infected with some disease was held in quarantine for 40 days, which allowed enough time for almost any disease to incubate and make itself known.

One of the first quarantine laws for plants was passed in 1911 to keep Med fly-infested fruit from Hawaii out of California. In the first year of inspections at one quarantine office in San Francisco, 1,828 parcels of fruit fly-infested plants, many of them infested with Med flies, were taken from the baggage of ships' passengers and crew. This was an important demonstration of how effective these inspections can be.

**54**

*A member of the Department of Agriculture's Beagle Brigade with confiscated agricultural items. The Beagle Brigade is a group of dogs that sniffs out prohibited fruits, vegetables, meats, and plants at U.S. international airports. These foods and plants are not allowed into the country because they may carry insects and diseases.*

**55**

Like host-specific predator insects, insecticides made from bacteria and viruses can also be specific. They are made to kill one kind of insect, and they do no other damage. For example, some garden catalogs now advertise a bacterial tablet that will gradually dissolve in a pool or slow-running stream. The tablet is made up of bacteria that infect only the larvae of mosquitoes. The bacteria prevent the larvae from becoming adults and do not harm anything else in the water.

Traps baited with a mating pheromone from female Japanese beetles, for example, attract every male Japanese beetle from miles around. And male gypsy moths rush into traps baited with the alluring pheromone of the female gypsy moth.

Entomologists at Cornell University have learned to use an insect's alarm pheromone to protect plants. When aphids are grabbed off a plant by a natural enemy, they emit a warning chemical that causes the other aphids of the same species to leave that plant in a hurry. After years of experimenting, the scientists made an imitation of this alarm chemical that can be sprayed on a plant. The imitation pheromone keeps the aphids away for as long as they can detect any of the pheromone on the plant.

Whether they tend small plots of garden vegetables, thousands of acres of cotton or wheat, or enormous groves of fruit trees, most farmers look to biological controls to protect their plants. They want to target specific pests and diseases and avoid terrible side effects. They remember the sad lessons of DDT and other chemical pesticides that moved up the food chain and destroyed so many living things. And while no one can predict how any plan that interferes with nature will work out in the long run, carefully thought-out biological controls offer great hope for the future.

The battle between humans and insects will probably

continue forever. Some scientists say the trick is not to interfere with insects at work among other insects. If we leave them alone, insects can be their own worst enemies. The important thing is to learn to live together because no matter how we feel about insects, we need them to keep all the ecosystems of the world in balance.

# GLOSSARY

**antibody:** a protein produced by certain white blood cells that attacks foreign substances in the body.

**antivenin:** a serum obtained from the blood of an animal, used to treat poisoning by animal or insect venom.

**arachnid:** an eight-legged animal such as a spider, mite, tick, or scorpion.

**arthropod:** an animal without a backbone having a jointed body, jointed legs, and an exoskeleton.

**biotoxin:** a poison produced by a living animal.

**carrion:** the dead or decaying flesh of an animal.

**complete metamorphosis:** a change in an animal's form, where the larva looks nothing like the adult; the animal goes through four stages: egg, larva, pupa, and adult.

**controlled conditions:** procedures followed in scientific experiments, often performed in a laboratory, to ensure that the materials and samples are not contaminated and the results are accurate.

**dose:** the amount of a substance, such as a medicine or poison, that will have an affect upon the recipient.

**entomologist:** a person who specializes in the study of insects.

**entomology:** the scientific study of insects.

**exoskeleton:** the hard or leathery outer covering of an insect that protects the insect and supports its muscles; an exoskeleton is shed, or molted, as the insect grows.

**genetics:** the study of heredity and the variation in animals and plants of the same or related kinds.

**grub:** a soft, thick, wormlike larva of an insect.

**hemotoxin:** a poison that breaks down blood vessels and red blood cells.

**heredity:** the passing of characteristics from one generation of plants and animals to the next.

**immunity:** resistance to a disease or poison.

**incomplete metamorphosis:** a change in an animal's form, where the adult looks similar to the larva; the animal goes through three stages: egg, larva (nymph), and adult.

**larva:** the wormlike young form of an insect; may be a grub, maggot, or caterpillar.

**malaria:** a usually fatal disease characterized by chills, fever, and sweating; transmitted by the bite of the *Anopheles* mosquito.

**microorganism:** an organism too small to be seen except with a microscope.

**neurotoxin:** a poison that affects or destroys nerve tissues such as the brain or spinal cord.

**nymph:** the stage between the egg and adult in the development of some insects; it resembles the adult but does not have wings.

**parasite:** an organism that lives on or in another organism from which it gets its food.

**pheromone:** a chemical produced by an animal to stimulate a response in another animal of the same species; a pheromone can attract a mate or signal for help.

**poison:** a substance that can cause illness or death, even in small amounts.

**pollination:** a form of reproduction carried out by insects, birds, and the wind in which the male organs (pollen) are transferred to the female parts of a flower or plant.

**predator:** an animal that lives by preying on other animals.

**pupa:** the resting, nonfeeding stage between the larva and adult in the development of some insects; most are enclosed in a tough case or cocoon.

**serum:** liquid obtained from the blood of an animal that has been made immune to a disease; used to prevent or cure the disease.

**spontaneous generation:** the belief that living organisms could develop from nonliving materials.

**toxin:** a poison produced by a plant, an animal, a bacterium, or a virus.

**venom:** the poison produced by an animal that is usually passed to a victim by a bite or sting.

**yellow fever:** a dangerous disease characterized by high fever and yellowing of the skin; transmitted by the bite of the *Aedes* mosquito.

# FURTHER READING

Blassingame, Wyatt. *The Little Killers (Fleas, Lice, Mosquitoes)*. New York: Putnam, 1975.

Greenbaker, Liz. *Bugs: Stingers, Suckers, Sweeties, and Swingers*. New York: Franklin Watts, 1993.

Lampton, Christopher. *Insect Attack*. Brookfield, Conn.: Millbrook Press, 1992.

Mound, Laurence. *Insect*. New York: Knopf, 1990.

Owen, Jennifer. *Insect Life*. Tulsa: Usborne, 1985.

Peissel, Michael, and Missy Allen. *Dangerous Insects*. New York: Chelsea House, 1993.

Pringle, Laurence. *Killer Bees*. New York: Morrow Junior Books, 1990.

Tesar, Jenny. *Insects*. Woodbridge, Conn.: Blackbirch, 1993.

# INDEX

animals, 7, 12, 13, 23, 24, 26, 33, 34, 35, 39, 42, 46
antelope, 42
antibodies, 33, 40
anticoagulants, 44
antihistamine, 17
antivenin, 33
ants, 23
    harvester ants, 24
    leaf-cutter ants, 7
    red ants, 24
    tropical fire ants, 23, 24
    weaver ants, 7
aphids, 49, 53, 54, 56
    walnut aphids, 53
arachnids, 12
Aristotle, 8
arthropods, 12

bacterial and viral sprays, 53
beekeepers, 19, 20, 22
bee larvae, 7
bees, 11, 12, 15, 19, 20
    bumblebees, 19, 22, 23
    honeybees, 19, 20, 22
    killer bees (African honeybees), 20, 21, 22,
beetles, 11
    Japanese beetles, 50, 56
    vedalia beetles (ladybugs), 50, 51
biotoxin, 13
bites and stings, 12-14, 16-20, 22-25, 27-29, 31, 32, 36, 37, 39-44
bubonic plague (Black Death), 36, 37
butterflies, 11, 12, 24

carnivores, 26

caterpillars, 11, 12, 18, 24, 25
    caterpillar of the Io moth, 24
    gypsy moth caterpillars, 51, 53
    puss moth caterpillar, 24
    saddleback caterpillar, 24
    tent caterpillars, 49
Centers for Disease Control and Prevention, 40
centipedes, 29, 31
cockroaches, 29
cocoon, 12
colonies, 20, 50
cottony-cushion scale, 50
crops, 7, 8, 19, 49

DDT, 52, 56
DEET, 39
diseases, 8, 10, 12, 20, 36, 37, 38, 44, 46, 54, 56
*Dragon Hunters, The*, 48
drugs and medicines, 8, 26

ecosystems, 7, 57
eggs, 10, 11, 18, 38, 45, 46, 48, 51, 53, 54
Eisner, Dr. Tom, 10
Entomological Society of London, 10
entomologists, 10, 46, 48, 50, 53, 56
entomology, 8
exoskeleton, 12, 34

fleas, 10, 34, 35, 36
    Oriental rat flea, 36
flies, 8, 11, 29
    fruit flies, 10, 49, 54
    housefly, 46
    Mediterranean fruit fly (Med fly), 54
    screwworm fly, 46, 48

tsetse fly, 42, 43
forensic entomologists, 10
formic acid, 23, 24

giant water bugs, 25
Gorgas, Colonel William, 45
Graham, Frank Jr., 48
grasshoppers, 11

Hippocrates, 44
honey, 7, 15, 20
host-specific parasites, 53, 54, 56
Hubbell, Sue, 22

insecticides, 42, 53, 56
invertebrates, 7

Kitasato, 36
Knipling, Edward, 46, 48
Koebele, Albert, 50

larvae, 11, 12, 15, 18, 38, 45, 46, 53, 54, 56
lice, 12, 41
    body lice, 41, 42
    crab lice, 41
    head lice, 41
locusts, 49
Lyme disease, 37, 39, 40

malaria, 10, 44, 45, 46
metamorphosis, 11
mites, 12
Moffett, Thomas, 10
molting, 39
mosquitoes, 10, 11, 43, 45, 46, 56
    *Aedes* mosquito, 44
    *Anopheles* mosquito, 44, 46
    *Culex pipiens*, 44
moths, 11, 12, 24
    gypsy moths, 49, 51, 52, 52, 53, 56
    silk moths, 51
Mouffet, Lucille, 26
Mouffet, Dr. Thomas, 26

*Nature*, 22
nectar, 19, 20, 43
nests and hives, 15, 16, 18, 19, 20, 21, 22, 23, 24
*New York Times*, 8
nymphs, 11, 38

Pasturella pestis, 36
pesticides, 36, 43, 56
pheromone, 18, 23, 56
pheromone traps, 53
plague, 45

plants, 12, 13, 23, 24, 26, 49, 49, 51, 54
poison, 12, 13, 22
pollen, 7, 19, 20
proboscis, 43

quarantines, 53, 54
queens, 15, 23

rats, 36, 37
Redi, Francesco, 8, 10
Rocky Mountain spotted fever, 37
Ross, Dr. Ronald, 44

scavengers, 7
scorpions, 12, 31, 32, 33
silk, 7
sleeping sickness, 42
slugs, 26
snakes, 13, 14
social insects, 15, 16, 18, 19, 23
solitary insects, 18
spiders, 7, 12, 13, 14, 26,
    black widow, 27, 29
    brown recluse, 29
    Mexican red-kneed tarantula, 27
    pink-toed tarantula, 27
    tarantulas, 18, 19, 26, 27
spirochete, 39, 40, 41
spontaneous generation, 8
stylets, 43, 44

Texas cattle fever, 37
ticks, 12, 37, 38, 39, 40
    seed ticks, 39
toxins, 13, 14
Trouvelot, Leopold, 51
trypanosome, 42
typhus fever, 41, 42

U.S. Department of Agriculture, 22
U.S. Public Health Service, 38

venom, 12, 13, 14, 17, 19, 20, 21, 22, 23,
    24, 25, 26, 27, 28, 29, 31, 32, 33
    hemotoxic venom, 14, 17, 27, 29
    neurotoxic venom, 14, 17, 27, 29, 33

wasps, 12, 14, 15, 16, 17, 18, 53
    hornets, 15, 16
    tarantula hawk wasp, 18, 19
    yellow jackets, 15, 16, 17
wax, 7, 20
weevils (snout beetles), 49
worms, 7, 8

yellow fever, 44, 45